A Gift of Faith:
An Amish Christmas Story
By
Sarah Price

Published by Price Publishing, LLC.
Morristown, New Jersey
2012

The Pennsylvania Dutch used in this manuscript is taken from the Pennsylvania Dutch Revised Dictionary (1991) by C. Richard Beam, Brookshire Publications, Inc. in Lancaster, PA.

Amish Photography on Cover Provided by S. A. Genung

Copyright © 2012 by Price Publishing, LLC.
All Rights Reserved

No part of this book may be reproduced in any form or by any electronic or mechanical means, including information storage and retrieval systems without permission in writing from the author, except by a reviewer who may quote brief passages in a review.

Contact the author at on Facebook at
http://www.facebook.com/fansofsarahprice or
visit her Web Blog at http://sarahpriceauthor.wordpress.com.

Price Publishing, LLC.
Morristown, NJ
http://www.pricepublishing.org

Books by Sarah Price

The Amish of Lancaster Series
#1 Fields of Corn
#2 Hills of Wheat
#3 Pastures of Faith
#4 Valley of Hope

The Amish of Ephrata Series
#1 The Tomato Patch
#2 The Quilting Bee
#3: The Hope Chest (2013)
#4: The Clothes Line (2013)

The Amish of Lititz
Plain Fame
Plain Change (2013)
Plain Again (2013)

Amish Circle Letters
Miriam's Letter: Volume 1
Rachel's Letter: Volume 2
Leah's Letter: Volume 3
Anna's Letter: Volume 4
Lizzie's Letter: Volume 5
Sylvia's Letter: Volume 6
Lovina's Letter: Volume 7
Ella's Letter: Volume 8
Mary Ruth's Letter: Volume 9
Miriam's Package: Volume 10

The Adventures of a Family Dog Series
#1 A Small Dog Named Peek-a-boo
#2 Peek-a-boo Runs Away
#3 Peek-a-boo's New Friends
#4 Peek-a-boo and Daisy Doodle

Other Books
Gypsy in Black
Fields of Zombies: Or How to Not Catch the Grunge Bug (with Sam Lang)
Postcards from Abby (with Ella Stewart)
Mark Miller's One Volume 11: The Power of Faith

Dedication

Writing a book is not a one-person operation. I would be remiss if I did not take a moment to thank several people for this Christmas novella.

First, my grandmother, Sarah Marie, who was my guiding light when it came to learning about the Mennonite and Amish faiths. From her, I learned that there is much more to these amazing cultures than what we see in movies or read about in books. She taught me about God but she also taught me about people. She gave me the depth of faith.

Secondly, I must thank my parents: Stanley and Eleanor. They gave me a spiritual foundation along with wings to fly and let me march to my own drum during my life. Without doubt, they taught me the breadth of faith.

But most of all, I must thank the most special person in my life and the cornerstone of my writing career: my husband, Marc, who helped with the script for this book and supports me with all of my other literary endeavors. He taught me many things about faith, things that go beyond depth and breadth. He taught me that different faiths can co-exist in harmony and work in peace together. Indeed, he taught me the power of faith.

Thank you all!

Table of Contents

Prologue

August 27th, 9:15pm

It all happened in the blink of an eye. The older man never saw it coming, but, in that short moment, his life would change forever.

The night was warm and the air muggy; the stars were twinkling way high in the sky, in-between the leftover clouds from the earlier rainstorm. There was a remnant of fog covering the road as was often the case in late August when it had rained earlier. The buggy's lights cast a weak halo on the road, reverberating on the windshield and half blinding the driver. His vision had seriously deteriorated over the last few months, the bishop thought and he decided to have it checked by the local doctor. Mayhaps a good pair of glasses would improve the situation.

As he pulled out of the farm's driveway, Jonas tried to remember where the series of potholes and the adjacent wide rut bordering a length of Samuel's front field were located. He had mentioned them before to the local Public Works department but lack of funds and the fact that this was a secondary road mostly used by Amish made it unlikely that fixing these was on the top of their priority list. That was for sure and certain, he thought. In fact, it hadn't even been touched since last winter.

Inside the buggy, the bishop and his wife sat quietly. Neither spoke. It was late and they were tired. The man wanted to get home to sleep. The woman had a lot on her mind. It had been a long, emotionally grueling day. They dealt with their inner turmoil in their own way.

"Whoa," the man said softly, hearing a car approaching

9

from behind the buggy. That road was winding, with curves and dips. He knew that the car would have trouble seeing them if the driver wasn't paying attention.

But the horse had picked up a fast pace and, when the man tried to pull the buggy over to the side of the road for the car to pass, a wheel found the rut and it got caught. The jerking motion of the buggy caused the horse to spook. It shied forward and, with that single motion, lurched in the opposite direction than the one that Jonas had intended it to take.

The impact of the car and the buggy broke the silence with a noise that no one else heard.

And then it was silent.

Chapter One

The house was quiet. Too quiet for Jonas' liking. The air seemed still and lifeless, heavy with oppression and isolation. It hung thick, giving him too much opportunity to think and to remember. Yet, as much as he disliked the silence, he had come to appreciate it for the very same reasons that he despised it: He needed to think and to remember. Doing so was his self-imposed penance and he had learned to live with it.

Outside, the wind blew against the windows. The glass vibrated, just a soft noise that broke the silence. In the distance, he could hear the rattle of a buggy's wheels and the familiar clip-clop of the horse's hooves pulling it down the road. For a moment, Jonas shut his eyes and listened. A memory flooded back to him and he smiled, but just for a brief second. As quick as it happened, the smiled faded along with the noise of the horse and buggy that was moving further down the road.

Once again, silence befell the room.

Frowning, he sat in the overstuffed blue chair, his wrinkled hands pressed together and resting atop the worn, brown leather Bible that lay upon his lap. Bits of torn paper and crocheted bookmarks in a variety of color poked through the top of the pages, marking favorite passages and sections of the holy book. But Jonas didn't open the Bible. Instead, he merely stared out the window, not seeing the greyish-blue sky and skeletons of leave-less trees that dotted the hillside.

He had always disliked winter. Even as a child, he dreaded the gloomy months that brought shortened days, uninspiring skies and freezing cold air. Seventy years later, that feeling had not changed and this winter was no different. His aging, thin skin seemed impacted by the cold air even more this year. He often wore his black jacket, even in the house. Nothing seemed to take the chill from his bones or, for that matter, from his heart.

But that wasn't surprising. Not this winter.

"Getting ready for tomorrow's sermon, Daed?" a voice said from the doorway, breaking the silence.

Jonas blinked and repeated his son's words in his head. *Ready? Sermon?* Then it dawned on him. He had forgotten it was Saturday evening, forgotten that tomorrow was a church Sunday. He felt his heart flutter inside of his chest, that all too familiar tightening that reminded him of his own inner darkness. The shadows of his mind weighed upon him like a rock pressed against his throat.

Slowly, he glanced over his shoulder at the door that separated his part of the house from where his son, Timothy, resided with his family. It didn't seem like it was that long ago when Jonas and Barbara had lived there, raising their own eight children. Now, the children were grown and seasons continued to change. Only five years ago, Barbara had convinced Jonas to move next door to the smaller grossdaadihaus so that Timothy could raise his family in the larger dwelling.

"What's that?" Jonas said gruffly.

Timothy crossed the small room in four easy strides. Jonas heard him, rather than saw his son as he had turned to look back out the window. "Reading, ja?" He sat down in the chair next to his daed, reaching out to touch his father's knee, forcing him to turn his eyes away from the gloomy outdoors and focus on the here and now. "It's gut that you are reading the Bible again. Mayhaps you can preach tomorrow."

"*Nein, nein,*" Jonas said abruptly, a scowl on his face as he waved his hand dismissively through the air. "Not reading. No preaching neither!" He was gruff and annoyed. He hadn't wanted company. Not tonight, anyway.

"Daed," Timothy said gently. "You need to…"

Jonas shook his head, interrupting his youngest son. A scowl crossed his face as he snapped, "Don't say another word, Timothy." Gently, he set the Bible on the floor next to his chair and then he stood up, reaching out to steady himself on the back of the chair. "I don't want to hear talk about what I need to do," he said sharply. "Not today. Not tomorrow."

Slowly, Jonas walked over to the kitchen counter. His feet shuffled on the linoleum floor. His knees ached from age and coldness. But the pain was welcomed, something that gave him pleasure. If he felt better and more energetic, he'd feel guilty. Pain made him feel right with God.

Reaching the counter, he opened a cabinet. It took him a moment to realize that it was the wrong one. He opened another until he found a plastic cup. He could feel his son watching him as he filled it with water from the faucet.

"Lydia wants to know if you'll join us for supper this evening," Timothy finally said, breaking the silence.

"*Nein*," Jonas replied. "I'm not hungry."

"You have to eat," Timothy pleaded. "You're wasting away."

Again, Jonas dismissed him with a wave of his hand. The truth was that he didn't want to go next door. Not now, not ever. Seeing young Benjamin was too much for Jonas, a reminder of past decisions gone wrong; decisions that haunted him. The child's hallowed eyes, pale face, and bruised skin were like tiny daggers poking at his heart. The boy looked so weak, so worn out. No child should have to undergo the pain of disease, especially one as deadly as leukemia.

"Mayhaps tomorrow evening, ja?" Jonas offered, knowing full well that he'd say no again if asked, too.

Timothy took a deep breath, clearly frustrated with his daed. Besides not wanting to break the fifth commandment, he knew better than to argue with him. His daed would win. He had for years. After all who, even his own son, could possibly win an argument win with the bishop of the church district.

"If you insist on being stubborn," Timothy said. "Not much I can do, I reckon. Not much more than to continue to pray for you."

Jonas snorted. "Lots of good that'll do you. Or me for that matter," he snapped, his eyes narrow and dark.

A new chill covered the room and Timothy knew that this conversation was over. There was no more room for discussion about the sharing of fellowship together. Not knowing what else to say, Timothy stood up. "Shall I lighten the lamp for you, then?"

"*Nein,*" his daed snapped.

Silence.

"Then I best be heading back to the supper table," he said, hanging his head and walking toward the door. He passed the clock on the wall and saw that it wasn't moving. Time stood still in Jonas King's house. Timothy knew better than to wind it. The first and only time that he had tried to wind the clock, his daed had crossed the room faster than a dog after a rabbit in the fields. He had shoved Timothy away and screamed at him, telling him to never touch that clock. No one ever mentioned it again.

Standing at the door, Timothy glanced back at his father, a shell of the man he used to be, leaning against the counter and staring at the wall, seeing nothing and feeling nothing. "Good night, Daed," Timothy said quietly, his heart heavy with grief for his father, as he slipped through the door.

Chapter Two

She was beautiful. That was the only thing Jonas could think as he stared at her. She wore a light green dress that highlighted her eyes, eyes that sparkled as she sang at the youth gathering. She was surrounded by a group of young women, but not one of them stood out like this beautiful Amish woman. It was as if a light shone down upon her, an aura, blinding him from seeing any of the other women. Her skin was golden brown, an indication that she was used to spending time outside, probably helping her daed in the fields. Her hair was so dark that he thought it was completely black. What little he could see shone from beneath her prayer kapp. And those eyes...sparkling green with a glow of life that intrigued him.

Earlier that evening, Jonas had joined the neighboring youth group with his cousin, Jeremiah. He had driven his buggy in the afternoon after services took place within his own church district. He had spent the late afternoon hours talking with his cousins as they sat on the porch drinking meadow tea and snacking on homemade chips. When Jeremiah had asked him to attend the singing, Jonas immediately agreed. It was nice to meet new people and sing the hymns in a new barn. It wasn't that he was tired of his own district. Nee, that wasn't the case. He was just looking for something different.

When his eyes fell upon the young woman singing in the middle of the youth group, he knew that he had found it.

"Who is that?" he asked Jeremiah, nudging him slightly with his elbow.

"Who?" Jeremiah asked; then, following Jonas' eyes, he replied: "Ah, ja! That's Barbara Yoder." He looked at Jonas and

smiled. *"Right pretty girl, ja?"*

Jonas repeated the name in his head, wondering if she was possibly related to several other Yoder families from his own district. Yoder was a popular name but he had never seen this young woman at any of the Yoder farms in his community. *"Is she...?"* He didn't finish the sentence, letting the question hang between them.

Jeremiah chuckled and lowered his voice. *"She's not spoken for, as far as I know,"* he said. *"But I also haven't heard tales of her courting much at all."* Jeremiah lowered his voice so that no one else could hear when he said, *"She's a quiet, godly girl. Good family, strong faith. Good luck, ja?"*

But Jonas knew that luck would have nothing to do with it. It was as if God had whispered into his ear that he was staring at his future wife. It was as simple as that.

During the brief break between singings, Jonas gathered the courage to approach Barbara Yoder. He carried a small cup of meadow tea and walked toward the group of three young women standing by the bales of hay that lined the side of the barn. No one seemed to notice him. Clearing his throat, he took a final step so that the group had no choice but to part for him to join them.

He smiled at the other women but his eyes quickly fell back upon Barbara Yoder. *"Thought you might be thirsty,"* he said, feeling as awkward as he sounded. He had never approached a woman before this evening. He wasn't certain how it was done. But he wasn't going to be too shy about it.

"Danke," she said, lowering her eyes. *"But I have one already."*

His neck felt hot and he feared that the color was rising to his cheeks. He hadn't noticed that she was already holding a cup in her hand. *"Do you have a ride home after the singing already, too?"* he blurted out and immediately hated the way it sounded. *Too coarse, too demanding. His heart pounded inside of his chest. Please God, he prayed. Don't let me have ruined my chance.*

She lifted her green eyes and stared at him, studying his face. At first, her expression was timid and concerned. Surely, she had noticed the abruptness of his question and she may not have liked it. He couldn't blame her. He was ashamed of how he had sounded. His heart raced and he quickly said his silent prayer to God again.

But, as she stared at him, something changed within her eyes. The concern disappeared, replaced with a look of clarity. She smiled at him, her face lighting up and her eyes sparkling. "Perhaps it would be best to introduce yourself, ja?" she said softly.

The two girls standing next to her quickly backed away, one of them trying to suppress a giggle as she was pulling her friend by the hand, leaving Barbara alone to talk with the young Amish man from the neighboring church district. It felt like the unchoreographed dance of a new courtship.

"Jonas King," he said, stumbling over his words. "My cousin told me your name already."

"Did he, now?" She continued smiling. "I suppose that was kind of him."

Jonas lifted his chin. "Said you are a godly woman."

Her smile faded, just a little. "No more so than anyone else, I suppose."

"I should like to find out," he announced boldly. "So may I take you home after the singing, Barbara Yoder?"

It was only a short hour later when he sat beside her in his buggy.

But to him it had seemed like an entire evening spent waiting for that moment. She seemed small and petite next to him and he had to make certain to press himself against the right side of the buggy so that he didn't brush against her. It was hard, especially since he was a large, burly man, even at twenty-two years of age.

After he made sure that she was comfortably situated, he opened the front windows, lifting them carefully and latching them overhead. It was a warm night, despite being early June. He glanced at her but she was staring straight ahead. No words passed between them as he clicked his tongue and slapped the reins on the horse's croup. The buggy lurched forward and began to roll down the lane.

Jonas didn't know where she lived and paused at the end of the farm's driveway where the singing had taken place. She pointed to the right and he turned in that direction. They didn't speak. The longer the silence hung between them, the harder it was for him to break it. This isn't going well, he thought glumly.

At the stop sign, she pointed to the left and he directed the horse in that direction. He wanted to say something, anything. But he couldn't. His lips remained shut and his words frozen inside of his head. There were so many questions that he wanted to ask but the silence was too thick and hard to break.

When she finally pointed to a mailbox on the side of the road, he pulled down the lane but stopped the horse when they were just off of the road. She looked at him, silently questioning why they had stopped.

"Barbara," he finally said. "That wasn't a good start to getting to know you."

"No, it wasn't," she admitted, but with a kind voice.

"I'd like to come calling this week," he said, feeling somehow encouraged. "Perhaps go for a buggy ride and some talk."

She hesitated, if just for a short moment.

He held up his hand. "Before you say no, I need you to understand that I haven't done this before," he admitted. "But, if you can have faith and forgive me for my inadequacies, mayhaps you might find that I strive to be a godly man. God willing, I hope to find myself a wife who has the same aspirations so that we might share a future together and raise a family that lives the Word of God."

She laughed.

For a moment, he was stunned. Laughing? He felt angry inside, embarrassed that she would actually laugh at him when he was trying to speak his heart. "You find that funny?" he asked, an edge to his voice.

"Oh Jonas," she said, shaking her head, laughter still lingering on her words. "You certainly tell it like you see it, ain't so?"

He was confused. "Is there any other way?"

She gently laid her hand on his arm, the gesture taking him by surprise. "I would look forward to having you come around to take me for a buggy ride this week," she said. Then, without saying another word, she slid open the door and climbed out of the buggy.

Peeking back inside, she smiled. "I'm sure glad that your cousin told you my name, Jonas King." Then, as if in an afterthought, she pointed to the sky. "Look, Jonas. A shining star, brighter than all the others. Always seems to be God shining down on us, ain't so?" She smiled before she turned and hurried down the driveway, disappearing into the darkness and eventually into the farmhouse.

Jonas had looked up at the sky, staring at the star for just a few moments. It was brighter than the other stars and, now that her words echoed in his mind, he, too, realized that the shining star could, indeed, be God smiling on them.

Chapter Three

The barn was crowded for the service. Jonas felt that familiar tightness in his chest as he walked through the line of women, briefly shaking each one's hand. He hated seeing the sorrow in their eyes as they greeted him. Each gaze spoke the same words, the same feelings of sympathy, sympathy that he neither wanted nor asked for. When he had finished passing through the line, he stood off to the side, waiting for the other ministers to join him.

The worshipers would enter the worship area, in a well-orchestrated and well-rehearsed order, the eldest among the women leading the way. These would sit on the hard wooden benches. Next, the older married men would enter and sit opposite these women. Then the younger, unmarried women would enter the room and sit behind the married women. Finally, the younger unmarried men would take their places along the walls.

Jonas sighed heavily, watching the progression as he had done hundreds of times throughout his years. In the past, he had looked forward to Sunday services. Lately, however, he longed to return to the comfort of his blue chair and the quiet of his empty house. There was no longer any comfort from the Lord for Jonas in the crowded barn with voices that lifted in unison as they began to sing a hymn from the Ausbund.

"Come," Jonas said to the other ministers and they walked to another room, away from the people singing. They would spend the next fifteen minutes praying and determining who would preach the sermon. Jonas knew that he would be praying that it would be anyone else but him. How could he stand before the congregation and preach when all he had in his heart was hatred and self-pity?

"Are you ready to preach today?" Amos Miller asked gently, his eyes staring at Jonas. The other men watched, a hopeful expression on their faces.

Jonas ignored the look as well as the question.

The three other ministers stared at Amos. They were at a loss as to how to handle their bishop. For three months, he had refused to preach, refused to speak about the hurt in his heart, and refused to discuss the fact that he had become lost. No one knew what to do with a bishop who was no longer willing to lead the district.

Time, they whispered to each other. *Give him time.* But Christmas was coming and the bishop always gave the Christmas sermon. As each church service passed without any indication that Jonas was healing, the ministers began to wonder how much time would be needed.

"I pray for you," Amos finally said, placing a hand on Jonas' arm. "I pray that you find your faith again."

The statement was met with silence; like so many before it.

It was decided that Amos would preach the first sermon and Stephen would preach the longer, following sermon. The ministers stood in a circle, holding each other's hands as they bowed their heads and prayed silently to God. Each mans' lips moved, except for Jonas who, despite holding the hands of the two men beside him, stared at the floor instead of shutting his eyes. Prayer eluded him.

"Bishop," someone called out as he was heading toward his buggy.

He had tried to leave without much fanfare. He never liked lengthy goodbyes. Instead, he had simply slipped out the door, hoping that no one spotted him. He didn't want to hear the question about how he was he doing or when could he join them for supper. All he wanted was to get home and be alone. Jonas stopped walking but didn't turn around. Whoever wanted his attention was running up behind him. No need to turn back, he told himself.

When she stood before him, he had to adjust his eyes before he recognized her as Rebecca, his brother Samuel's wife. "Service is over," he said. "You don't need to call me bishop." He ignored the frown on her face. "What is it?"

"Samuel asked that you come by this evening," she said. There was a deep sadness in her eyes. Jonas couldn't imagine why. "We would like to share supper with you."

Supper. It was always about food, he thought crossly. He waved his hand dismissively. "*Nein, nein,*" he mumbled. That was all? He couldn't be bothered with social visits. Not now. Maybe not ever.

She reached out and grabbed his arm. "We need your help," she pleaded.

"With what?"

"It's Eli," she whispered. "He's so withdrawn. It's been months and it gets worse with every passing week."

Jonas shook his head. "There is nothing I can do for him," he snapped impatiently. "Why ask me?"

"You *are* our bishop," she stated. "And you *are* Samuel's oldest brother. He stood with you at your wedding. Barbara was my best friend and truest sister." Rebecca refused to budge. "She would have wanted you to help Eli."

A chill went through his spine. For a moment, he was angry. How dare she suggest that she could possibly know what Barbara would have wanted! He had spent almost fifty years with that woman. No one knew Barbara better than he did. And certainly not Rebecca. Yet, at the same time, a whisper brushed his ear and he heard the words that haunted him: *Forgive and have faith.* He wasn't certain where they came from, just deep in his memory bank. Whenever he heard them in his head, he tried to remember where they came from. But he couldn't. He just knew that they had something to do with Barbara.

"I'll ride over at four," he said firmly and walked away from Rebecca, furious with himself for having given in but knowing that the whisper in his ears was a sign that Rebecca was right: Barbara would have wanted him to help his nephew.

When he entered the house, Samuel and Rebecca were seated around the table. Samuel was four years younger than Jonas and had married in his late twenties. Eli was the last of his children that remained at home, a strapping twenty-year old that was clearly absent from the small family gathering. Jonas frowned, wondering why he had been invited if Eli wasn't even there.

"*Guder Owed,*" he said without conviction as he removed his hat, hanging it on the peg on the wall before he walked toward the table.

Samuel stood up and reached for his brother's hand. "Jonas, I cannot thank you enough for coming," he said, a nervous smile on his face. Clearly he felt uncomfortable but supported at the same time. "I was really relieved when Rebecca said that you agreed."

Jonas sat down at the head of the table. There were small allowances for the bishop. That was one of them. "What seems to be the trouble?"

His brother shook his head. "It's Eli," he started. "I don't know what is bothering him but he's moving further from God, of that I'm sure and certain."

A soft puff of air indicated Jonas' reaction, as if mocking Samuel for having brought him to the house. "And you want me to do what about that, *Bruder*?"

Rebecca took a sharp breath of air and answered for her husband. "You *are* our bishop, Jonas. Whether you are suffering or not, you were chosen by lot and we need your guidance." She paused and glanced at Samuel. "Eli needs your guidance."

"I don't have much to offer," Jonas said meekly, with a simple shrug of his shoulders.

Rebecca lifted her chin. "I don't believe you," she said defiantly.

"Rebecca," Samuel chastised softly, reaching out to touch her hand. He gave it a gentle squeeze then turned to his brother. "We do need your help, Jonas. Eli has always looked up to you. Mayhaps you can talk to him. Find out what is wrong."

"It's those boys!" Rebecca snapped. "Those Englische boys he's always running with. They are turning him sour during his *Rumschpringe*!"

Fergevve un heb glauwa. The words whispered through his ears. He blinked his eyes, surprised. Where had that come from? Was it Barbara sending him yet another sign?

"Where is the boy?" Jonas said reluctantly.

"I'll call him down for supper," Rebecca said, jumping up from her seat and hurrying to the bottom of the stairs. She disappeared, leaving Samuel and Jonas alone for a few moments.

Samuel looked at Jonas and sighed. "How is Benjamin? I didn't see him at service today."

Jonas shook his head. He knew the question was coming but hated to be asked. How could he explain how he felt about losing Barbara on the very day that he had heard about Benjamin? "It doesn't look promising," he admitted, his voice catching. "Timothy and Lydia took him for the chemotherapy. The boy was deathly ill and that Englische medicine didn't seem to work none."

"Isn't there anything we can do?"

"Nothing we can do," Jonas said. "The doctors have suggested a bone marrow transplant but the chances of finding a match are clearly impossible. Timothy is willing to permit the transplant but who would possibly donate? There has to be a DNA match."

Samuel caught his breath. "I'm so sorry, Jonas. Such a shame," he said. "Please extend my condolences and prayers to the family."

Jonas clenched his teeth. He knew what was unspoken between them. He didn't need to be reminded of that decision so long ago. He shut his eyes and was about to say something, reminding Samuel about the circumstances from that day, so many years ago but his thoughts were interrupted.

"What are you doing here?" the voice said from the stairs.

Jonas turned around, surprised to see Eli standing at the foot of the stairs, his face pale and drawn. The twenty-year old had lost weight. A lot of weight. He had dark circles under his eyes and a look of severe depression. Jonas frowned. When was the last time he had seen Eli? An image flashed before him, a split second of something that tugged at his memory. But, as soon as he started to see it, it was gone. It must have been months. The funeral, he thought. His eyes had been large and deeply frightened, staring at Jonas from the crowd. Yes, Jonas told himself. It must have been at the funeral.

"That's not a kind way to great your *Onkle* and our bishop," Rebecca scolded as she walked down the stairs behind her son. "He's come to talk to you."

Eli wrapped his arms around himself and, at his mother's urging, crossed the room to the table. "Don't have nothing to say," Eli mumbled, reluctantly sitting down as far away from Jonas as he could and refusing to make eye contact. He kept his arms folded across his chest, as if hugging himself.

"What's troubling you, Eli?" Jonas prodded. It was clear that the young man was in trouble.

"Don't have nothing to say," he repeated softly, his eyes down, as if talking to himself.

Jonas exhaled and glanced at Samuel. *Rumschpringe,* he thought. Clearly the youth was mixed up with someone or something that was troubling him. "You given much thought to baptism yet, Eli? Haven't seen you at services recently." As soon as the words popped out of his mouth, Jonas realized that it was true. He hadn't given much thought to Eli not being at church for weeks…perhaps months. He frowned. Yes, Eli had been missing and, until this very moment, he hadn't fully realized for how long.

"Not getting baptized," Eli said, his voice cold and flat.

Rebecca gasped and covered her mouth with her hand. "Oh Eli!"

Even Samuel leaned forward, shocked at his son's admission. "Don't say such a thing!" he hissed. "Not in this house. Not to the bishop!" He paused. "Not to your parents."

Eli jumped to his feet. "What does it matter anyway? My life is over!" he shouted and started to run to the door.

"Eli!" Jonas called out, his deep voice booming and stopping the young man in his tracks. Slowly, Jonas arose from the chair and walked over to Eli who stood with his back toward him. He placed a hand on his nephew's shoulder. "Your life is not over. Don't say such a thing. I lost my wife. I miss her each day. Now, my grandson is dying. He's only eight. He will never have what you have before you. A life. A future. A choice. God has a purpose for you. Don't waste it."

Eli tensed. "Where is God?"

For a moment, Jonas asked himself the same question. It was the question he had asked himself repeatedly, every day for the past three months: *Where was God?* God took Barbara. God was taking Benjamin. Could God be so cruel as to take Eli, too? With faith he did not feel, Jonas said, "God has a plan for every one of us, Eli. Whatever trouble you are in, whatever fears you face, God walks beside you. Remember Job and the troubles that he was given by Satan. Even then, God protected him." There was a spark, a small glimmer of something that tingled inside of his heart. Was it possible to actually believe that again? He wondered. *Save this boy,* he found himself praying.

"I don't like God's plan," Eli said sharply and darted out the door, leaving his mother near tears and his father in shock.

Jonas stared after him, watching his silhouette disappear around the side of the barn. How could he argue with his nephew? Wasn't he feeling the same way? God's plan for Barbara and God's plan for Benjamin certainly weren't what Jonas had anticipated from the Lord, the God that he had served without any question for the past seventy years. He lowered his shoulders and sighed. He had no words of comfort. Not for Eli. Not for his parents. And especially not for himself.

Chapter Four

When he finally had the courage to ask her to marry him, he knew deep inside that she would say yes. They had spent the past three months courting, taking a weekly buggy ride every Wednesday evening and another one home after bi-weekly singings. They courted in private as was the custom among the young people. No one needed to know that Jonas King was calling on Barbara Yoder. It was between the two of them. They enjoyed it that way.

It was late in September when he finally asked her. October was around the corner and he wanted to be one of the first in his community to announce their engagement. It would be a short engagement, merely three weeks. Just enough time for the families to plan the meal, assign the duties and invite the friends to celebrate the joyous occasion.

He slowed the buggy down as they drove along the winding country road. The sky was black, another moonless night with stars twinkling above their heads. He smiled when he saw the one star, a bright star, directly overhead of an evergreen tree alongside the road. "A star," he whispered.

She smiled. "God shining on us."

"Or smiling," he said. He pulled the buggy to the side of the road and he noticed that she glanced at him, surprised that he had stopped it. But, as usual, she didn't question him. A right gut woman, indeed, he thought.

"Barbara," he said, clearing his throat. "You have impressed me with your godly ways."

She frowned, just for a moment. "Indeed?"

"Ja, indeed," he repeated her word and lifted his chin as he continued. *"I find you a most honorable woman. Your faith in God is admirable."* He paused but she didn't say anything. He was glad. If she had, he might have hesitated, losing track of his speech. *"I hope that I have proven myself to be just as honorable, a man of strong faith and godliness. I believe that we could share a life together, worship God and raise a family. If you agree, I'd like to have the bishop announce our intentions at the next service."*

She smiled at him, her eyes dancing. *"I should like that very much, Jonas King."*

And with that said, they were set to be married.

The wedding took place the second Tuesday of October. It was the first wedding of the season and over 300 people attended. The day seemed like any other church day to Jonas. He rose early in the morning, dressed in his regular black Sunday suit, and rode over to the Yoders' home with his younger brothers, Samuel and David. The rest of the family had left earlier, his mamm packing the buggy full of freshly baked bread and pies.

She was wearing a light blue dress, her face shining and bright, as her eyes met his across the room. He kept a stern face, knowing that it was a serious day, almost as serious as the day he had taken his baptism. Unlike other couples, Jonas King was not about romance and love. He was about commitment and God's Word. Yet, despite his determination to remain serious and focused on God, he felt a warmth in his heart when they stood before the bishop after the three hour service. And, when they were finally wed, he prayed for forgiveness for the moment of pride he felt about this beautiful, godly woman beside him that he could now call his wife.

For the next few months, he spent the weeks at home, helping his daed and brothers with the farm chores. On the weekends, he would drive his buggy to the Yoders' to pick up his bride. They would visit relatives, spending time on their farms until Sunday evening when he would bring her home to her parents' farm. Back then, it was the way of the Amish. Short visits during the weekends until the spring when he would finally pick her up one last time to bring her home to their own farm.

It had taken him a while to find a farm, a place to call home with Barbara. It wasn't until February when he had learned that an older Amish man was selling his 80-acre farm, just a town over from his daed's. Without discussing it with Barbara, Jonas purchased the farm, sight unseen by his young bride. Whatever was wrong with it could be fixed, he reasoned. God had led him to the farm and he wasn't about to risk losing it to another family.

She never questioned his decision and seemed happy enough when he moved her to their farm in April.

The lot was chosen just a week after he turned forty-five. Four years earlier, he had been selected to become a minister in the district. Now, he led it. Jonas had wept when he saw the small slip of paper that fluttered his selected Bible. It fluttered to the ground in front of the congregation, a silent announcement that he was chosen from the district's ministers to be their next bishop.

It had only been a month before when they had buried Yonie Esh, the bishop of only twenty years. He had been sixty, too young to die. He had donated a kidney to his brother. It was a decision that had not been made lightly. The result was that both Yonie Esh and his brother, Jacob, had died: the bishop from an unexpected staph infection that attacked his heart and his brother *from going into toxic shock after his body rejected the organ.*

The church district was lost, moving about like ghosts. They had been so hopeful that the transplant would work. They had prayed long and hard about whether or not to permit it. It seemed like playing God and many in the district were unhappy about it. Now, their beloved bishop was dead and they had to move on, feeling the guilt of the community's decision to permit Yonie to donate his kidney without understanding the ramifications of such a decision.

One of Jonas' first orders of business was to spend time speaking with the congregation about the issue of donating blood and organs. It wasn't too hard to come to the conclusion that their district would forbid it. With two widows and two fatherless families, the issue was embraced by all. Better to let God decide, they said. If a donor could be found among the Englische, perhaps that would be permissible. But not from within the community. It was simply too dangerous, too close to interfering with God's will. It was simply not meant to be.

The first test of that decision came six months after Timothy was born. One of the older members of the community had kidney failure. It was so similar to Jacob Esh's condition that the community felt the wounds open once again. But Jonas stood firm. No donors from within the community. Within three months, the man died. No one blamed Jonas. Indeed, they praised him for his commitment to God in his role as a bishop. God first, they agreed amongst themselves.

It was nine years later, however, when the next challenge came. A farming accident left young Gideon Fischer hospitalized. He had numerous surgeries but, his liver was damaged. All that he needed was a portion of a liver from a matching donor. The family was willing to step up and be tested to see if they might possibly be

34

that donor but Jonas quickly reminded them about the community's decision almost ten years past. Some in the district frowned and mumbled that it was time to rethink the decision. After all, medical knowledge had made great strides in the ten years since Yonie and Jacob Esh had died. But Jonas stayed firm, not willing to lose more members of the community.

Gideon Fischer died two months later, never having returned home from the hospital.

The decision haunted Jonas. He saw the boy's face every time he looked at his parents. He prayed for guidance from the Lord, hoping that he could forgive himself. Had he made the right decision? Had he done all that he could?

"Jonas?" Barbara asked as she handed him a steaming mug of hot chocolate. "You feeling alright tonight, ja?"

He shook his head. After so many years together, she knew him too well. She could read his body language, sense his mood. She was a good wife in all ways. "Nein," he said.

"Gideon?" she asked.

He nodded.

"Forgive and have faith," she whispered and reached out to touch his hand. "A wise man told me that once, so many years ago."

He smiled. "Yes, I remember that," he said slowly. "I wasn't very eloquent, wasn't I?"

"No," she said. "But God whispered in my ear that you were the one."

He twisted in his seat and stared at her. "What did you just say?"

Her green eyes danced at him. "I never told you, did I?"

He shook his head and that made her smile even more. "Ja, God whispered in my ear to give you a chance. He told me that you were the chosen man for me."

"I'm not certain how I feel about that," he said, frowning. Would God truly have talked to her? After all these years, why hadn't she told him this? Would it have mattered?

She laughed. "Don't be questioning it, Jonas King. But rejoice that I felt His hand in our matchmaking. Whether it truly was God or merely a crazy young woman enamored with a very nervous young man trying to ask her to ride home with him, I'm quite pleased with the results." She patted his hand. "And you should be, too. We've had a good life and still have oh so many blessed years of joy ahead of us."

That had been the plan: To watch their family expand with the addition of grandchildren and great-grandchildren. To celebrate Christmas and Easter each year. To grow old together. It had never been in their plans for one of them to die.

Chapter Five

Jonas heard the buggy pulling down the driveway and, with a deep sigh, forced himself to get up from his chair to walk toward the kitchen counter. He lifted the shade and peered outside, not surprised to see Samuel and Leah. What did surprise him was that they did not walk toward his front door but the door that led to the main house. Clearly, they were planning to visit with Timothy and Lydia about young Benjamin.

Letting the shade fall back into place, he stood alone in the darkness. He liked it dark. It felt like warm arms shrouded him, comforting him as he listened to the depth of the silence. He dreaded being interrupted by his *bruder,* but he knew that they would certainly stop in to see how he was doing and to update him on Eli.

Better to kill two birds with one stone, he thought. If he went over to Timothy's house, he could leave when he wanted, thus cutting the visit short. Plus, he knew that he couldn't continue to avoid Benjamin forever.

When he entered Lydia's kitchen, the four adults looked up in surprise. They were seated at the kitchen table, their heads bent together as if in prayer. But his presence startled them.

"*Wie gehts?*" he asked, shuffling across the floor.

Timothy jumped up from his seat. "Daed! We were just praying for you!"

For me? Jonas scowled. "Don't waste those prayers on me. Should be praying for your *kind,* ain't so?" He ignored the look that passed between Timothy and Samuel. Glancing around the room, he noticed that the adults were alone. "Where are Benjamin and the other *kinner*? Thought I'd visit with all of you at once."

Lydia stood up and hurried to the stove to pour Jonas a cup of hot coffee while Timothy gestured to the empty chair at the head of the table. "Sit, Daed. We have something to tell you," he said solemnly.

Grunting, Jonas took his time walking toward the table. Prayers for him? Something to tell him? He didn't like the direction this unexpected visit was headed and he immediately regretted having come over.

Once Lydia had set the mug before him, she returned to her place next to Timothy, staring hopefully at her husband. Timothy took a deep breath and started talking. "We are taking Benjamin to the hospital. We fear that his time is near," he said. "Without a donor, there is nothing else we can do but to keep him comfortable."

"He'd be more comfortable here," Jonas snapped but refused to meet their eyes.

Lydia dabbed at her eyes with a white handkerchief. "I had hopes that he'd be home for Christmas but he's suffering too much."

Samuel lifted his chin and leveled his gaze at his father. "Of course, you could lift the ban on donors, Jonas."

And there it was. The reason for the prayers. The reason for wanting to talk to him. The reason Samuel was there.

Slamming his hand on the table, Jonas pushed his chair back. His coffee spilled over and Lydia jumped up to grab a dishtowel. The liquid ran down the table and started dribbling onto the floor as Jonas began to shout, "I knew it! That's what this is about, ja? You'd have me make special favors and change our Ordnung for your own purposes?" He stood up. "What kind of bishop would I be?"

Samuel tightened his lips and said, "You haven't been much of a bishop these past few months."

"Samuel!" Leah gasped.

"It's true," Samuel snapped back, brushing his wife's hand off his arm. "Walking around in self-pity, refusing to preach, unable to help his own family! One quick decision, one word of support and that boy could be saved!"

Jonas glared at him. "God has a plan for all of us and I will not presume to play God. I'll not change the Ordnung for my own grandson. We didn't change it for Gideon Fischer! If God intends for Benjamin to live, He will provide a donor that will be found outside of the church."

"You know that's impossible," Timothy said. "We were told it had to be a genetic match!"

"*For with God nothing shall be impossible[1],*" Jonas quoted from the Bible as he lifted an eyebrow. "Isn't that what you believe?"

"It's what you are supposed to believe, too!" Samuel shot back at his brother.

Jonas started walking toward the door. "I did believe it," he said, his voice soft and low. "But you're right, not anymore."

---

[1] Luke 1:37

Chapter Six

They first noticed the issues with Benjamin when he was six years old. He was tiring too much. When he did play, he would fall a lot and he bruised easily. When little red marks began appearing under his skin, Timothy and Lydia approached Barbara about it.

"Have you ever seen anything like this?" Lydia asked, her voice a whisper.

"Nee," Barbara said, staring at Benjamin's arm. "Have you talked to the doctor then?"

Lydia shook her head. "I thought it would pass but it just keeps getting worse."

It was decided that they would take Benjamin to the local doctor in town. Barbara insisted on riding along. She held Benjamin's hand while they waited in the outer office, too aware of the strange looks from the Englische children and their parents. Lydia filled out the paperwork the receptionist gave to her, thankful that Barbara had come along.

"I want him to have some blood work done," the doctor said, a sad expression in his eyes.

"What are you thinking?" Lydia insisted, realizing the look of worry on his face.

"I won't know until the blood work comes back," the doctor replied, deflecting the question, the answer to which he already seemed to know.

Barbara placed her hand on the doctor's arm. "We need to know what we are dealing with. Is it something serious?" Her green eyes stared at the doctor, pleading with him for some indication of what was wrong with Benjamin.

He sighed and held his file close to his chest. "I don't know for sure and I don't want to alarm you but it appears to be acute myelogenous leukemia."

Both Lydia and Barbara frowned.

"Acute what?"

The doctor sighed. "Bone marrow cancer."

From that point forward, their lives had changed. Doctor visits, rounds of chemotherapy and lots of community prayers for Benjamin became an integral part of their lives. After the first round of chemotherapy, there was hope that he was in remission. But, when he turned eight, it began again, the symptoms even worse than before.

"Benjamin needs a donor," the doctor said. He was sitting behind his big mahogany desk, his crisp white jacket showing off his summer tan. Behind him were photos of golf courses and family members. It was a sharp contrast with the lives of the four Amish people seated before him. He tapped his fingers on top of the manila folder on his desk. "And that donor would have to be a family member. To match his DNA. There is no other choice"

Timothy and Lydia stared at the doctor while Jonas and Barbara stood at the back of the room, offering their support as best they could. At the news, Lydia lowered her head into her hands and began to weep. Timothy paled and stiffened at the news.

"We don't permit donors from within the church," he whispered.

The doctor nodded slowly as he said, "That's what I suspected."

"Is there no chance that an Englischer might be a suitable donor?" Timothy asked, hope in his voice.

"Not for this type of cancer, I'm afraid."

The ride home from the doctor's office had been quiet. No one knew what to say so they rode in silence. Jonas had hated that silence. It was too loud, indicating the depths of despair that everyone was feeling. Jonas knew that Timothy and Lydia were struggling with that decision from so many years ago, the one that they were probably praying he would overturn. But how could he? How could he change his own ruling about being a donor? Wouldn't the community see him as a weak bishop? Willing to change the Ordnung for his own grandson, despite the death of Gideon Fischer?

The Mennonite driver dropped the four of them off at Samuel's farm as Leah had offered to watch the kinner. The sun was beginning to set behind the tree line. The meeting with the doctor had taken longer than expected and, now, they had to spend some time in fellowship with Samuel and his family. After the light supper, the children played with the kittens in the front yard while Eli watched them. Leah had asked him to keep them occupied so that the adults could discuss the situation without children overhearing.

"Is there nothing we can do then?" Samuel said.

"Nee," Timothy replied, his face pale and drained of color. "It's a donor or..."

Lydia choked back a sob.

Jonas exhaled loudly. "It's God's will," he said sternly. "If the boy is chosen to go home to the Lord, we should be singing His praises, not questioning His decision."

Barbara laid her hand on his arm. "Jonas," she said softly.

"I know what you are thinking," he said angrily, staring at his son. "But it wouldn't be fair to the Fischer family. They lost a son, too."

"Times are different now!" Timothy blurted out. "Please Daed, consider lifting the ban on donors."

"Nein!" He lifted his hand up, palm outward. "Does not the Bible say: 'For I know the plans I have for you, declares the LORD, plans to prosper you and not harm you, plans to give you hope and a future[2].' We are taught to accept those plans without question."

He stood up, angry that his word had been questioned. After all, he was the bishop and he was the final say-so. He left the kitchen, needing the fresh air to cool his head. The night was starting to close in around the farm and he found himself comforted in the darkness, as if the arms of God were wrapped around him whispered, "You made the right decision."

When he finally turned around to walk back toward the house, he failed to notice the brilliant star that was just over the horizon, shining down on the growing crops in Samuel's fields.

---

[2] Jeremiah 29:11.

Chapter Seven

It was Friday, the day before Christmas Eve, when Timothy burst through the door to his house. Jonas heard him long before the door slammed open. After all, he was shouting from the top of his lungs, "Daed! It's happened! It's happened!"

Jonas had been switching between napping in his favorite chair and staring out the window at the tall evergreen tree that grew by the barn. Snow was falling and covering the tree with a light dusting. With the overcast sky and the white fields behind the barn, it was a pretty scene. Perfect for Christmas and absolutely opposite to how he felt.

When Timothy started shouting, awaking him from his trance-like mood, it took Jonas a minute to realize that something had indeed happened. The sleepiness in his head immediately disappeared as he realized that it could only mean one thing. Benjamin! He felt that familiar tightness in his chest. Had the boy passed? He knew God to be cruel but to do that just before Christmas?

"Dear Lord," he whispered, shutting his eyes and shaking his head. "Not the boy."

As soon as the words came out of his mouth, he realized that it was the first time he had actually offered a prayer in months. It felt odd to pray to God after months of fighting Him.

Jonas turned in his chair, reluctant to greet his son and have to deal with comforting others or arranging another funeral. Yet, as soon as he looked at Timothy, something did not make sense. There were no tears on Timothy's face and his expression was full of excitement. Lydia hurried through the door and, instead of looking sad, she was smiling. In fact, her face glowed with joy. Jonas looked back at Timothy, confused. Clearly they were both overwhelmed with good news.

"What is it?" Jonas asked, his voice catching in his throat.

"A Christmas miracle!" Timothy cried out, lifting his hands in the air. Lydia laughed and let Timothy hug her.

Jonas stared at them, certain that they had lost their minds. "What are you talking about, son?"

"A donor!" Timothy sank to his knees by his father's chair and reached for his hands. "They have found a donor!"

"What do you mean they have found a donor?" Jonas asked, his eyes wide and bright.

Lydia sank onto the sofa, tears now freely streaming down her face. "The doctor left a message on the phone this morning. We only just received it now and called back. He told us the good news. Someone has actually donated blood that matches Benjamin's DNA!" She clapped her hands together and lifted her eyes to the ceiling as if thanking God.

"Who?" Jonas demanded.

"An Englische man!"

None of this made sense. "But…"

"I know!" Timothy laughed. "It's crazy. The doctor couldn't believe it either! They said it was a perfect match!"

Silence set in the room for a few moments.

"Impossible!" Jonas said, his voice incredulous with disbelief.

Timothy pointed at his father, his smile widening on his face. "Nothing is impossible! '*The things which are impossible with men are possible with God.*'³ Isn't that so?" He embraced his wife again, not caring that his father was watching. "Thank you Lord for this amazing miracle!"

It was Christmas Eve and the family had traveled the three miles to share the family meal at Samuel's farm. They always shared a large Christmas Eve meal with the extended family, reserving the Christmas meal for smaller celebrations. In years past, it had been held at their farm as they had the largest gathering room between the two kitchens. Barbara would make a large meal on Christmas Eve so that, on Christmas Day, they could spend time with the family. Her holiday menu was always the same: Different types of chicken and beef, mashed potatoes, yams, applesauce, canned beets, corn that had been frozen in the summer, and fresh baked bread. And no one could make a better pumpkin pie than his Barbara.

However, this year, without Barbara to help with the meal, it was easier for the family to gather at Samuel's where Leah and her daughters-in-law could prepare the food. It was just one more reminder about how much he missed Barbara and how his life would never be the same.

Hesitantly, Jonas walked into the kitchen, aware that everyone was congratulating Timothy and Lydia for the good news about Benjamin. He watched the joy on their faces, the tears in the eyes of the women, and his heart fluttered in his chest. God has truly intervened, he thought. It was as if God was reprimanding him for not having changed the ban on medical donations. Every time he heard that word, "Congratulations", his chest tightened a little more and he sank further into despair. It was as if they had done something personally to save the child, he grumbled to

---

[3] Luke 18:27

himself.

Feeling the weight of guilt on his shoulders, Jonas moved away from the crowd. He wasn't certain why he felt so angry. In truth, he knew that he should be happy. Benjamin, his own grandson, finally had a chance. Another round of chemotherapy and then the bone marrow transplant could possibly see him in remission. It would be wonderful to see him run and play with the other kinner. Barbara always loved hearing the children playing in the barnyard. She could sit for hours on the porch, crocheting pretty placemats or wall hangings as she listened to their laughter.

His heart fluttered inside of his chest and he reached up to rub it. Barbara wasn't going to be there to see Benjamin run and play ever again. Feeling weak, he removed himself to the back of the room where the sofa and chairs had been pushed aside to make room for the numerous tables that would accommodate the fifty people who were celebrating Christmas Eve supper.

He was sitting in a chair by himself, thinking back to the previous year's Christmas. How could he have not known that it would be their last? Why hadn't God warned him? He felt that familiar anger from within as he longed for just one more day to be with his wife. If only he had been driving slower. If only he had left a few minutes later. If only…

"Jonas!"

His thoughts interrupted, he dropped his hand from his chest and looked up. Samuel was hurrying toward him, laughing as he leaned down to hug his brother.

"It's a joyous day, *Bruder*!"

Jonas nodded his head but said nothing.

"It's a *wunderbaar gut* day to celebrate the birth of Jesus!"

This time, Jonas replied, "Gut to have the family together, I reckon."

"Congratulations about the mysterious donor!" Samuel said, changing the subject. "What a glorious gift from God! A true miracle!"

Jonas didn't know what to say. Did he believe it was a miracle? Why would God grant one with Benjamin but not with Barbara? "I reckon," he said, looking around the room. He noticed Eli leaning against the wall. His face was pale and he was standing with more weight on one leg than another. "Your boy doing well, then?"

Samuel's expression changed as if a dark cloud had passed over his head. "Thought he was doing better. Seemed to be staying home more but I suspect he's still running with those Englische boys," Samuel said, pulling up a chair next to him. He leaned over and lowered his voice. "Didn't come home the night before last." He shook his head. "And feeling poorly as well. Says he slipped on the ice and hurt his hip."

Jonas frowned. Ice? "You don't say?" He turned his eyes and stared at Eli. There was something odd about the way he was standing there. Truly in deep pain but forcing himself to be a part of the festivities. *Like me*, he realized. It was at that moment that Eli's eyes traveled the room and met Jonas'. For a split second, something flashed in Jonas' memory. A similar moment but he couldn't place where or when. He was looking up, staring into the distance and saw someone staring back. The same eyes. The same expression. And then it dawned on him.

This time, his chest tightened and he gasped. In doing so, he realized that he couldn't breathe. His heart was fluttering again, palpitating inside of his chest in what felt like irregular beats. His blood raced through his veins and he suddenly felt very hot. The room began to spin and he was on the verge of fainting. But not before he saw Eli rush toward him, calling out, "We have to help him!"

And then, the room went black.

Chapter Eight

August 27th, 8:45pm

The bishop and his wife were preparing to leave Samuel's house. They were drained, emotionally, physically, and spiritually. It had been a long and hard day with disappointing news and even more disappointing discussions.

Timothy and Lydia had left earlier, taking the kinner home to get them to bed. But Jonas and Barbara had stayed later, talking privately with Samuel and Leah. For a while, they debated the issue of reversing the ban. Samuel did his best to sway his brother into changing his ruling but Jonas had remained firm in his convictions. To reverse the decision would inflict unnecessary pain on the Fischer family, he said. After all, the decision hadn't been reversed for Gideon. How would they feel if Jonas changed it now for his own grandson? They'd never forgive the church, he said while he was really thinking: I'd never forgive myself.

Barbara hadn't said much during the discussion. She sat quietly by Jonas' side and played with the edge of a paper towel that was on the table. She didn't meet his eyes which typically meant that she didn't agree with his decision but respected his wisdom enough to not argue.

Leah also remained silent but Jonas could tell from her body language that she supported Samuel in his hope to see the decision reversed. Of course she would, he thought ruefully. Everyone is thinking of the immediate issue, not of the long term benefit to the community.

Jonas and Barbara said their goodbyes and left.

Chapter Nine

We have to help him!

Jonas blinked his eyes, trying to make sense of where he was. He tried to sit up but found that he was not in his own room. He was in a strange bed in a strange house. The noises were different, the smells were different. And there was light. Soft, filtered light coming from a window in the door. It dawned on him that he was at the hospital. He felt at a loss. A hospital? He swung his legs over the edge of the bed, frowning when he realized that they were bare. He was in a hospital gown. Where were his clothes?

The fog lifted from his head as the images of Christmas Eve swarmed through his memory. The family gathered at Samuel's house. The strange smells of an unfamiliar Christmas Eve supper. The joy in Samuel's voice at the good news about Benjamin. The strange gaze on Eli's face when he lifted his eyes and met Jonas'. What had happened? What had made him faint?

We have to help him.

Eli's words reverberated in his ears. He had heard those words before last night. He had heard that same voice say them before, too. It had been at that moment that he knew. The pieces came together and, with complete clarity, he knew what Barbara had meant. *Fergevve un heb glauwa.* It was the moment of truth.

"Mr. King! You need to lie back down and rest," a soft voice said from the doorway.

He looked over his shoulder and saw a young woman in a green hospital uniform. She was a blond woman and her hair was pulled back into a short ponytail. She smiled at him and hurried to the bed, lifting the covers so that he could swing his legs back on the mattress. But he pushed her hand away.

"I have to leave," he demanded.

"Oh I don't think that's going to happen," she said gently, reaching for the blood pressure band and wrapping it around Jonas' arm.

He glared at her. "I'm the bishop. It's Christmas morning and I need to get to my church to preach," he snapped as if she should know that.

"Well, you can't just get up and go," she said, her voice firm now, pumping the bulb. He felt the band tighten around his upper arm and she pressed her fingers on his wrist, quiet as she released the pressure. Satisfied, she removed the band and tucked it back in the rack on the wall. "You have to wait to see the doctor," she added.

Jonas crossed his arms over his chest. "Why am I here?"

"Wait for the doctor," she repeated, her voice a bit too sing-songy for his liking.

"I'd like to know what happened!"

She smiled and shook her head. Clearly she wasn't about to budge on this argument. "The doctor will be in soon to discuss it with you," she said. "It's not my place."

"Did I have a heart attack?" he demanded.

"Mr. King, I'm sure this is most distressing for you but you need to calm down and relax. It's not good for you to get so worked up," she responded, her eyes as sharp as her tone. He was surprised at how quickly she could fluctuate between soft and gentle and firm and strong. "Now you just wait until the doctor gets in. He'll be in early for his morning rounds and I'll make certain to let him know you are most anxious. It won't be long and he will answer all of your questions."

It was seven-thirty when the doctor walked through the door. Jonas was sitting in the same spot with his arms still crossed over his chest. He had spent the past hour trying to replay everything in his mind: Yonie Esh, Gideon Fischer, Barbara King, and Benjamin King. It all made sense, the thread that wove those lives together. He had to get to the church service, he had to explain to everyone what he had learned.

"Mr. King," the doctor said, pulling a pen from his pocket and glancing through a metal file that he plucked from the foot of Jonas' bed. "I hear you are most anxious to leave us," he said. "I suppose I understand that, being Christmas and all." He looked up and smiled over the top of his black rimmed glasses. "Merry Christmas, by the way."

"I need to leave," Jonas replied.

"Yes, I heard about that," the doctor said as he bent his head over the file. He flipped through several pages and pursed his lips, nodding his head to himself. "You gave everyone quite a scare yesterday. But I'm happy to say that your EKG shows no coronary distress and your blood work came back healthy as could be." He looked up. "Have you been feeling stress, Mr. King?"

"Of course!" he snapped. "My wife died and my grandson is gravely ill."

"I see," the doctor said, scribbling on the file. "Terribly sorry to hear that, Mr. King."

"If it wasn't a heart attack, what was it?" Jonas asked.

The doctor looked up, peering at Jonas from behind his glasses. "Anxiety," he said. The word sounded severe and Jonas frowned as the doctor continued. "Anxiety can manifest itself in different ways in your body. Headaches, chest pains, even stomach aches. Losing your wife and having an ill grandson would certainly create high levels of stress."

The doctor shut the metal chart and slid his pen back in his breast pocket. "Under normal circumstances, I'd want to keep you in the hospital for observation. Just for a day or two, especially at your age." He held up his hand to stop the protest from Jonas before it began. "However, I understand your desire to go home, to be with your family, especially on Christmas Day. But I'm sending you home with some medicine and I want you to see your local doctor during the week. Just for a check-up."

It took another two hours to finally get the paperwork and release forms signed. It was just before ten o'clock when the nurse wheeled him to the front entrance of the hospital where a taxicab was awaiting him. He hadn't even bothered to call his Mennonite driver to pick him up.

It was Christmas, after all.

Chapter Ten

August 27th, 9:41pm

For a moment, Jonas felt as though he were floating. Time seemed to stand still as his body moved through the air. There was practically no noise, except for the buzzing sounds of some far away cicadas calling for new mates... But even these, the pastor could not hear. Just a deep silence. It was as if his mind had turned off the sounds of the horse screaming, Barbara crying out, and the buggy shattering against the car. He heard nothing, just sensing the blood rushing through his veins and his heart pounding inside of his chest. Silence.

When the buggy came to a rest, it was resting on its side. The door had flung open and Jonas was surprised to see that Barbara wasn't beside him. Sound slowly returned to him, his senses turning back on. He blinked, trying to understand what had just happened. A car accident, he realized. The horse. The buggy. His wife. He managed to push his way out the warped, opened door on Barbara's side of the buggy. Of course, he thought. He must have blacked out for a moment and she already had freed herself from the buggy.

There was light on the road coming from the headlights of the car. He paused and looked around. He could see four people inside the car. He shuffled toward it, his head spinning and aching. "Barbara?" he called out as he lifted his hand to cover his eyes, shielding them from the bright glow of the headlights reverberating on the fog and the wet road.

He heard her groan and realized she was behind him. Turning, he searched the darkness but he could see nothing. "Barbara?" he called again.

"Jonas," she said, her voice barely a whisper.

He glanced at the car. No one was moving. The doors were shut and the front of the car on the passenger side was dented. "Help me!" he implored, his voice shaky as he moved in the direction of his wife's voice. "Help me!"

The driver side door opened and a shadow emerged. Another followed from the rear of the car. But no one walked toward him to assist with Barbara.

She was lying on the road, crumpled in a heap. Jonas ran to her, ignoring the pain that shot through his legs and back. Kneeling beside her, he noticed that there was blood on her head. Too much blood. He cradled her in his lap, covering the wound with his hand.

"Get help!" he called out, holding Barbara as tight as he could without moving her. She coughed and he could hear that she was having a difficult time breathing.

"They be fine. Let's get out of here," a man's voice, tainted with a slight Deitsch accent said from the darkness near the car.

"We have to help them!" another voice said urgently. Then, as if trying to sound less panicky, he added, "It's a crime to leave the scene of an accident, you know."

"They fine, I said," the first voice snapped harshly. "Don't need no cops here and a DUI! Besides, Amish don't press charges or talk to cops. You know that!"

Jonas couldn't believe he was hearing those words. He turned his head, staring in the direction of the car. The driver got back into the car and, for just a split second, Jonas saw the other man, a young man, standing there in the shadow, watching him. But he was too far way to really see him. "Please," he pleaded, his eyes starting to swell with tears. If they drove away, it would be too late. Who knew when someone else might drive by?

But the car drove away, leaving Jonas alone in the dark with his wife on the side of the road. He hadn't even thought to check on the horse or the buggy. His only concern was his beloved wife, Barbara, who laid on the hard macadam, gasping for breath.

"Jonas," she whispered.

"Don't try to talk," he demanded, his voice cracking. Please don't take her, Lord, he prayed. He lifted his eyes toward the heaven, tears filling his eyes. He stared at the stars just over the top of a tall evergreen tree on the side of the road. Don't take her away from me.

"A star," she whispered.

"Barbara, please," he pleaded. "Keep your strength."

"There's a star over that evergreen," she said softly. "God is shining on us."

Jonas felt that God was doing anything but shining on them but he didn't say those words. Instead, he tried to silence her as he held her in his arms. Surely someone would come along to help them? Surely those boys couldn't just drive away and leave them on the road, Barbara injured and bleeding in his arms.

"Promise me something," she managed to say, heaving and ignoring his demand that she'd be still. "Promise me that when the time comes, you will do one thing."

Tears streamed down his face. She was dying. She knew it. They both knew it. It didn't matter how hard he prayed to God. God was taking his wife, right now, right at this moment.

"What is it, Barbara"

She clutched his hand and squeezed it as hard as she could. He could barely feel it for she had no strength. "Fergevve un heb glauwa[4]," she whispered. For a moment he didn't think he heard her clearly. But, before he could ask, she repeated it with as much conviction as she could master. "Fergevve un heb glauwa, Jonas, Fergevve un heb glauwa!"

She coughed again and, in the dim light from the buggy, Jonas could see blood streaming from the corner of her mouth. Those were the last words she would say to him. He clung to her, feeling the warm sticky sensation of blood on his clothing but not caring. Then, her body seemed to loosen, the blood stream ceasing as he felt her life slip away. All of a sudden he was surrounded by silence. Even the cicadas had become quiet. Jonas sensed a benevolent presence emanating from her limp body and slowly rising to rejoin with her Creator.

And, just like that, she was gone.

---

[4] *Forgive and have faith.*

Chapter Eleven

The air was thick and cold and it smelled like snow. Jonas sat in the back of the taxicab, feeling uncomfortable and anxious. He wished the taxicab could drive faster, he wished that he could slap the reins on the driver to speed up the car. He found himself pressing his feet against the floorboard as if he were driving a horse and buggy, subconsciously urging it forward.

He could hear them singing as he exited the taxicab. The lights of the farmhouse were lit up and the voices from within greeted him. He paid the taxi driver, pulling a twenty-dollar bill from his cracked, leather wallet. The driver thanked him, wished him a Merry Christmas, and then pulled out of the driveway.

For a long moment, Jonas stood there, breathing in the crisp winter air and listening to the words of the hymn, the Lob Lieb, that the members of the church sang:

> O God Father, we praise You
> And Your goodness exalt,
> With You, O Lord, so graciously
> Have manifested to us anew,
> And have brought us together, Lord,
> To admonish us through Your Word,
> Grant us grace to this.
>
> Open the mouth, Lord, of Your servants,
> Moreover grant them wisdom
> That they may rightly speak Your Word,
> Which ministers to a godly life
> And is useful to Your glory,
> Give us hunger for such nourishment,

That is our desire.

Give our hearts understanding as well,
Enlightenment here on earth,
That your Word be ingrained in us,
That we may become godly
And live in righteousness,
Heeding Your Word at all times,
So we will remain undeceived.

Yours, O Lord, is the kingdom alone,
And the power altogether.
We praise You in the assembly,
Giving thanks to your name,
And beseech You from the depths of our hearts
That You would be with us at this hour
Through Jesus Christ, Amen[5].

He stood in the doorway, tears in his eyes as he listened to the final words of the hymn. The silence that followed the hymn continued and no one from the ministers' bench stood up. For a moment, Jonas didn't understand why. Normally, this would be when the minister who was giving the main sermon would stand before the gathered families and preach. But, today, the room remained silent.

That was when he noticed that everyone was staring at him.

Slowly, Jonas removed his hat and, holding it humbly before him, he walked into the room and crossed to the center, the area between the divided benches. Women always sat on one side,

---

[5] Ausbund, Song 131. Also known as the *Lob Lieb*. It is sung at every church service as the second hymn. In an Amish church service, it would be sung in High German. The author has taken the liberty of using the English translation instead.

men on the other. For a Christmas service, there were also plenty of people standing along the wall. It was a full house, to say the least. And every pair of eyes was waiting.

For a short while, he shut his eyes and lowered his head, a silent prayer shared between himself and God. The people waited, their eyes lowered out of respect for the moment. They could sense the emotion behind Jonas standing before them, clearly seeking the strength to speak.

When Jonas lifted his head, he stared around the room. He took his time, looking at each face that was waiting with anticipation for what Jonas would say.

"*Fergevve un heb glauwa*," he said at last.

Silence.

"Those were the last words that my wife said to me four months ago when she died in my arms." He paused, turning his eyes to look at his son, Timothy. "Forgive and have faith," he translated. "She did not say those words once. Not twice. But three times." He held up his hand, showing three fingers. "Three times."

No one moved.

"I thought she was repeating words I said to her on the very day that I met her," he said, a hint of a smile on his lips. "Forgive and have faith. That's what I had said to her when I attempted to ask her to ride home with me from a singing. I reckon I did a poor job at that!" Another pause. "Truth is that I reckon that I've done a poor job of many things throughout my life."

He took a moment and looked around the room again.

"Forgive and have faith," he said. "I realize that she wasn't reminding me of my poor attempts at courtship. Instead, she was telling me what I would have to do in the future. I would have to forgive and have faith! And not once, not twice, but three times!"

His voice rose. "Three times!"

"First and foremost, I forgive you, God," he said, lifting his eyes to gaze at the ceiling. He held his hands out to the side. "I forgive You for having taken my wife in such a seemingly senseless accident. She left me long before I was ready to let her join You. You have a plan for us, each and everyone one of us. My life has been rich with love and happiness, bountiful pleasures in seeing sunrises and sunsets, hearing children's laughter and songs of worship. I never should have doubted You or lost faith in Your Divine Holiness."

Jonas took a deep breath and lowered his hands at his side. He stared at the floor and shook his head. "Secondly, I forgive myself," he whispered. "I forgive myself for having made poor decisions, for not giving Gideon Fischer a chance, for not understanding the seriousness of self-pride. That pride almost cost my own grandson the chance to live a full life. And it certainly cost Gideon Fischer his chance. I forgive myself for having lost faith in myself. I am but a man and prone to err in judgment."

One more pause. He held up his hand and counted off, "One is for God. Two is for me. Who is the third one for?" He stared at the three fingers as if contemplating the answer. For a moment, he frowned, studying his hand as if truly in wonder of the answer. But the truth was that he already knew.

"My grandson, Benjamin, needs a bone marrow donor. But our community agreed so long ago that we would not permit our own to donate," Jonas said and took a deep breath. "How could I change that ruling for my grandson when Gideon Fischer didn't have that option?"

Jonas turned toward Timothy. "My son told me wonderful news. Please, son, share the news with the congregation!"

Timothy stood and, with his hands crossed before his waist, he tried to contain his excitement as he spoke. "A donor has been found!"

"A donor!" Jonas repeated.

"A Christmas miracle!" Timothy added, his eyes falling upon his wife who sat across the room from him.

Jonas smiled. "Nothing is impossible through God, ja?" He waited until his son sat back down before he continued. "A true miracle indeed," he started. "For the bone marrow donor needs to have a genetic connection to Benjamin. That would seem to be the miracle…that a person outside of our community is a match!"

The congregation murmured softly to each other and Jonas waited, letting the noise grow for a few moments. Then, he held up his hand. "But that is not the miracle," he said. "Nein, the miracle began long ago. The miracle began the night that my wife was killed in that accident, the very accident that caused me to question my faith!"

The room was still.

"You see, the donor was in the car. The donor who had this miracle genetic match was in that car!"

There was a collective gasp in the room.

Jonas nodded his head. "Ja, it is true. You see," Jonas continued, pacing the floor. "It was the guilt over that accident that caused the donor to make the most supreme sacrifice. He went to the hospital and donated his bone marrow bone marrow to give a chance to my grandson, Benjamin. A chance I was not even willing to give him!" Jonas looked around the room. "If God had not taken Barbara from us, if that accident had never happened, my grandson would surely die! I wasn't going to permit anyone to be a donor, not if it meant questioning my own decision from so many years ago."

"But the genetic match?" Samuel said. "Surely that is a miracle, too?"

"Is it, *Bruder*?" Jonas smiled, a sad smile but there was compassion in his eyes. He stared around the room until his eyes fell upon his nephew, Eli. Holding up three fingers, he smiled as he said, "I forgive you, Eli King." He turned his hand slightly so that he was pointing at the stunned young man with all three fingers. "I forgive you for having been in the car that hit my buggy, the accident that sent my wife home to walk with the Lord."

There was more than one gasp from the congregation and several heads turned to look at Eli. The young man sat there, the color instantly drained from his face. It looked as though he wanted to get up and run from the room. But it was clear that it would not be easy to do such a thing. Instead, he stared at Jonas, panic on his face.

Sensing the young man's fright, Jonas paused and smiled, his face glowing. He turned to look out among the congregation. "Without that accident, Eli would never have felt the guilt that compelled him to donate his bone marrow. And we all have learned that it is a perfect match. God may have taken Barbara but, in exchange, He has given us a chance with Benjamin."

There was a soft murmuring of approval among the members of the church.

Jonas didn't stop. He continued preaching. "You see, I had lost my faith in God. I had lost my faith that God can truly work miracles. I was too angry and unwilling to remember that God does have a plan for each and every one of us. Who am I now to question those plans?" He paused, thinking for just a moment. "Who are we to question His plans?" he added, stressing the word *we.*

He lifted his hands up to the ceiling and shut his eyes. "Thank you, God. I stand before you, humbled and ashamed, that it took so long for me to give my heart in understanding and to see the glory of Your enlightenment here on earth. What a wonderful gift You have given me on this very special Christmas. For indeed, You have returned to me something that I had lost so very long ago."

He opened his eyes and stared at the amazed faces watching him. His own face glowed, radiating the love of the Lord. How could he explain this to the people, he wondered. But he knew that he would spend the rest of his life trying. "You see, God has given me a gift of faith!"

Then, walking over to the bench where his nephew sat, Jonas placed his hand on Eli's shoulder and stared down into his face. "Danke Eli for what you have done for young Benjamin," he said. "And *danke* for what you have done for me."

"I'm so sorry *Onkle*," Eli whispered, tears in his eyes.

"*Nein*," Jonas said. "The Lord took and you have given. My faith is restored and all are forgiven. Just as Barbara requested." Then, in the most unusual act, Jonas leaned down and put his arms around Eli, embracing him and letting his nephew's tears fall onto his shoulders, joining as they both publicly reconnected with their lost faith.

Epilogue

It was the day of the Spring baptism. Jonas stood before the congregation, eager to welcome in the young men and women of the church district that had gone through the Instructional. For the past twelve weeks, they had met with Jonas during church service for instruction about what baptism truly meant.

Now, as he stood before the group, two men and three women, Jonas tried to hide his smile. Today there was joy in his heart for among the group was Eli King.

He cleared his throat before he proceeded with the baptism. He started with the first question of the baptismal candidates by asking, "Is it your heartfelt desire to now receive holy baptism and do you believe that you are prepared for it?"

Five shaky voices said "Ja" as they nodded their heads.

Jonas gestured before him. "In God's name, I ask you to kneel down," he said and waited for them to do so. Then, placing his hand in the air over their heads, he continued. "This kneeling down is not to me but takes place before the Lord, the most High and all-knowing God who heads this church."

Silence. All eyes were on the candidates' backs. Only Jonas could see their faces.

"Do you therefore now believe that Jesus Christ is the Son of God, who came into the world to save repentant sinners?" he asked. He waited for each candidate to respond in the affirmative before he moved onto the second baptismal question.

"Can you then renounce the world, the devil, your own flesh and blood, and be obedient to God and His church?" he asked, staring at the five kneeling youths. Each held their hands before them, clasped in humility with their heads bowed down as they responded in a clear voice: Yes.

It was at this point that Jonas proceeded to pour water over the heads of each candidate, bestowing on them a final prayer. One of the other minister's wives stood beside him to help the women to their feet and give them the final baptismal kiss.

The last candidate to be baptized was Eli King. Jonas hesitated before he poured the water over Eli's head. He paused, just long enough for Eli to look up at him, concerned with the delay.

Jonas smiled at Eli, his heart filled with joy at his nephew as he said, "May the dear God who has begun the good work in you help to complete it. May He comfort you and strengthen you unto a blessed end, through Jesus Christ." He reached his hand down to help Jonas to his feet. Once standing before him, Jonas leaned forward and, as was required of the bishop, he kissed his nephew on the lips, a gesture of humility practiced among his people during baptism.

"May God bless you, Eli King," he whispered. Then, in a louder voice, he added as he looked around the room at the faces that stared at him, "Through Jesus Christ, we pray. Amen."

ABOUT THE AUTHOR

The Preiss family emigrated from Europe in 1705, settling in Pennsylvania as the area's first wave of Mennonite families. Sarah Price has always respected and honored her ancestors through exploration and research about her family's history and their religion. At nineteen, she befriended an Amish family and lived on their farm throughout the years. Twenty-five years later, Sarah Price splits her time between her home outside of New York City and an Amish farm in Lancaster County, PA where she retreats to reflect, write, and reconnect with her Amish friends and Mennonite family.

Find Sarah Price on Facebook and Goodreads!
Learn about upcoming books, sequels, series, and contests!

Contact the author at sarahprice.author@gmail.com.
Visit her weblog at http://sarahpriceauthor.wordpress.com or
on Facebook at www.facebook.com/fansofsarahprice.